the money experiment

The House Studio
PO Box 419527
Kansas City, MO 64141

Copyright 2012 by The House Studio

ISBN 978-0-8341-2734-0

Printed in the United States of America

Editor: Kristen Allen
Cover and Interior Design by J.R. Caines

thehousestudio.com

10 9 8 7 6 5 4 3 2 1

# the money experiment

A Community Practice in Financial Simplicity

**Ryan Pugh**

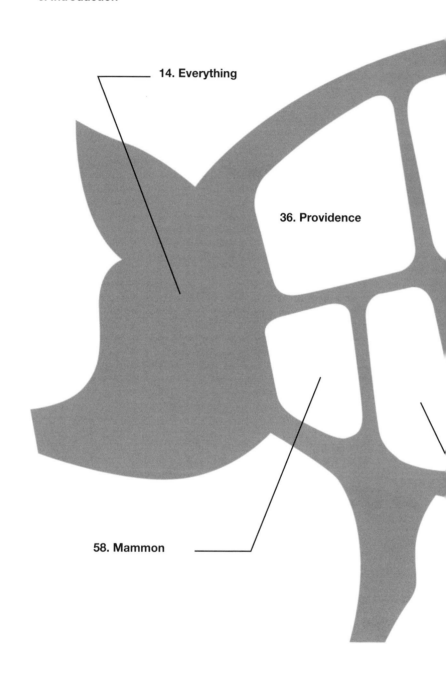

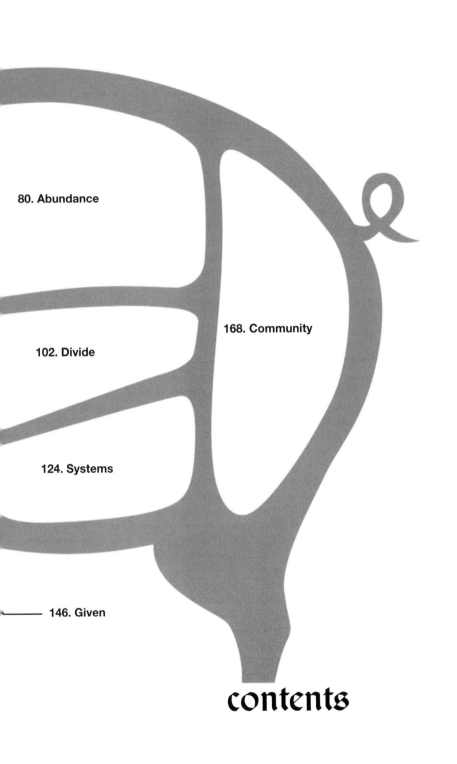

contents

introduction

People are okay having **faith**, so long as it doesn't alter their **life**. Trouble is, a faith that **doesn't** alter your life isn't **real faith**.

**Greg Boyd**

Even though money affects most everything we do on a daily basis, it just isn't one of our favorite discussion topics (unless it's asking that always fun "What would you do with one million dollars?" question or debating a solution to the financial downfall of the United States). We go to coffee shops and talk about God, and we go to church and talk about sports and shopping. But money doesn't really come up much in any discussion.

Maybe that's why so many pastors dread preaching about money. And why an overwhelming number of marriages begin without the individual parties ever discussing how they'll save—and spend—their money after they're married. Money talks make *everyone* uncomfortable. Think about it: if you really want to make a conversation awkward, just ask someone about the details of his or her bank account. Or, next Sunday, try peeking over the shoulder of the woman in front of you while the offering plate passes her by. Chances are, if she catches you looking, you won't find her sitting in front of you again.

Yet, as uncomfortable as talking about money makes us, money (and possessions) is one of the most talked about topics in Scripture. What we do with the resources with which we have been entrusted is inextricably linked to our relationships with God and others. Whether we have little or much, the way we view and spend money directly affects the way we view what God is doing in us and in the world. Our goal should be to spend our resources, both individually and communally, in ways that contribute to God's mission to restore the world to what it was created to be.

I believe that God meant it when he repeatedly saw and proclaimed the goodness of his creation in the first chapter of Genesis (verses 3, 10, 12, 18, 21, 25, and 31). I believe that humans once lived as the noble stewards we were created to be. Over time, though, we have chosen our own way. We've decided that we would rather *own* God's creation than lovingly care for it. We sought (and seek) possessions for ourselves instead of living in God's economy, an economy in which there is enough for everyone. The result is one we know all too well—a broken world, tragic suffering, and torn relationships.

But there is good news! God hasn't given up on his creation and has promised to make all things new. Every person. Every part of creation. God is a missional God and is searching for people to join his mission of restoring the world. All around the world, ordinary people are rising up to re-imagine the way they spend money around the mission of God.

So, with all that in mind, as we begin this journey together, here are a couple things this book is *not*.

There are surely some principles laid out in the book about how Christians are called to view and spend money, but this book is not a quick list of exactly what that looks like. It could be very easy to create tweets out of scriptures about money, trying to capture the significance of a verse or passage in 140 characters or less. Sometimes this approach works, but in using it, we often miss what the rest of the story is really saying.

This book is also not *everything* the Bible says about money. I'd like to think I've covered the most important parts and that these parts give a foundation upon which everything else rests. But chances are there is more (isn't there always more when God is involved?). So I hope you continue to wrestle with Scripture alongside others.

So, what *is* this book?

I love math. I love numbers and details. I have an analytical mind that naturally focuses on facts and evidence. Since I pay more attention to details, I haven't always been a stories guy, but I've come to realize that life is all about story, specifically God's story. It's all about placing our story into the grand story of God, from beginning to end, creation to restoration. This book is about what Scripture tells us about money and how stories and reflections from Scripture might push us to place our entire lives, our stories, including money, into God's story and mission. Some parts of the book focus on historical stories involving money. Some focus on parables Jesus told about money. And some focus on other scriptural expressions about money. But it all comes back to seeing everything through the lens of the story and mission into which we are called.

Specifically, I hope this book helps create conversations about how we can view and spend money in ways that cause us to participate in God's mission to restore the world to its intended wholeness. If we can't even talk about money, living into God's mission with our money becomes much harder—maybe even impossible. So I hope you'll talk, learn, grow, question, and take chances—all with the purpose of living into God's mission with your money and resources. Some of it may not be easy, and some of it may be uncomfortable. But it just might change your life.

# Let's begin here.

# it's plain and simple.

**1 Read and discuss a chapter.**

2 Each person chooses one of eight experiments to carry out . . . or make up some of your own.

**3 Journal your thoughts on our pages. (Why else would we give you so much white space?)**

4 Share your stories with the group next week.

everything

# And God SAW that it was good.[1]

Whether you are like me and grew up learning about the story of creation (see Genesis 1-2) on flannelgraph or you are new to all of this, it's easy to overlook these amazing words. Over and over again as God creates day and night, water and sky, plants and animals, men and women (all of it!), he steps back and proclaims how truly *good* it is. If we are honest with ourselves, we are hard-pressed to come up with the same reaction God had as he breathed creation into beautiful existence. When we look around our lives and our world, the brokenness, the ugliness, the pain, and the deep suffering are much more apparent.

The beauty and love that rest in God's creation have become muddied because we have chosen our own ways over God's perfect way. We have become owners instead of stewards, and the result is brokenness throughout creation. But the beauty and love have not been blotted out altogether—we see them all around us, too. We are capable of much harm, but the image of God in each of us, even a distorted image, still produces love and beauty, through the grace of God.

All of creation groans for the day when it will be restored and renewed to how it was created to be in the beginning. As Paul writes in Romans 8:18-25, creation waits in eager expectation for God's people to be revealed so that one day all of creation will be set free from its bondage to decay. There is hope! And it is this story of hope, restoration, and renewal to which God calls each of us to be a part as we work with God in what he's doing in and for our world.

If we are serious about this work—God's work of restoring and renewing each person and each piece of his creation—it becomes easier to see how every area of our lives is affected. From the beginning, Scripture reveals a wholeness in humans. Much differently, we often like to compartmentalize our lives. Physical life, spiritual life, mental life, emotional life. Or church life, work life, family life, school life, play life. It's easy for us to compartmentalize our lives, but if we look closely, Scripture doesn't make distinctions between physical and spiritual or church and work life. The gospel of Christ is concerned with the whole person, and God's love transforms our whole lives. We are called to (and get to) place ourselves into God's mission of restoration. As Jesus taught us to pray for things on earth to be as they are in heaven, we begin to see a kingdom coming to earth that doesn't change just the "spiritual" state of our hearts but our entire lives.

How we live—specifically, how we view and spend money (that is why you're here, right?)—is directly connected to our capacity to love God and love our neighbor. The fundamental confession that Scripture makes about money and resources is that "the earth is the LORD's, and everything in it" (Psalm 24:1). All throughout God's story, we are reminded that we don't *own* anything (as much as we think we do), that God created it all and therefore owns it all, and that we came into this world with nothing and will take nothing out of it (see 1 Timothy 6:7).

To live by this confession that everything is God's is the beginning of loving God and loving others as we throw ourselves into God's mission with all that we are and have, including money.

talk

In 1 and 2 Corinthians*, Paul calls us God's coworkers in the world. What does it mean to be God's fellow workers?

\* (1 Corinthians 3:9; 2 Corinthians 6:1)

We live in a society that thrives on a mindset of personal ownership.
How does the confession that everything is God's confront and contradict this worldview?

# Family dinner.

## (It doesn't have to be so old school.)

We get it. Families are pulled in every direction—work, school, sports, recitals. The list goes on. This week, make an effort to eat several meals together (or with friends if you don't live near your family). Pray before each meal, giving thanks for food and time together. As you pray and eat, remember those without food and without family.

**Journal your thoughts here.**

# That chicken wasn't made at the grocery store.

You may have bought your food at the grocery store, but where was it before that? This week, keep a list of all the food you eat. Then, reflect on where it originally came from. Were the animals raised well? Were the workers who harvested it and delivered it paid fair wages? Was God's earth cared for? Research local food stores that honor God's creation—and shop there.

**Push a pencil.**

# **Not** financial-advisor-recommended.

It's a good thing to have a budget, but some of us need to think deeper about what God wants our budget to look like rather than what we or even a "financial expert" thinks it should look like.

Create a monthly budget or take a hard look at your existing budget. Add, adjust, or delete altogether the items or categories that don't help you live by the confession that everything is God's or lead you into God's mission.

Tell the page what you think.

# 𝕬 loose grip.

The next time someone asks to borrow something, give it. Know someone who needs something that you have? Provide it. No questions asked.

**Do tell.**

# Creation restoration.

Scripture promises that all things are being made new. One day, every person and every piece of God's beautiful and broken creation will be restored and created new! Every act of creativity, compassion, justice, and love will be part of the new world.

Find something in your garage, yard, or neighborhood that could use some tender loving care. Maybe an old chair, a flower bed, or a piece of equipment. Imagine how you could restore the item to be beautiful and valuable again. Then do it. As you work, contemplate how God is restoring you today.

**Artists welcome here. Doodle away.**

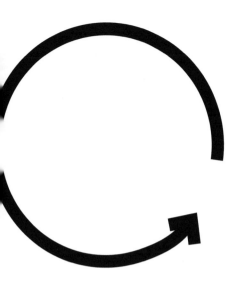

# One step at a time.

As the hands and feet of Jesus, we play a fundamental role in God's mission in and for the world. Even small acts can make a difference in our world being restored to its intended wholeness.

Visit www.mynextstepis.org, a place where people share what they want to do to help change the world, and submit your "next step." Involve money in your next step, whether it's simple or difficult.

**Drop a line. Or two.**

# It is the Lord's, after all.

Read and pray the Lord's Prayer (Matthew 6:9-13; Luke 11:2-4) each day this week. Try reading with fresh eyes, dreaming how you can work for God's coming kingdom as God's will is done on earth as it is in heaven.

**White spaces are meant to be filled.**

# It's not all about the Benjamins.

Yes, this book is about money. But *everything,* not just money, is from God. Life itself is a gift from God. Choose a person in your community who just needs to be with somebody. Give him or her the resource of your friendship. Meet this person for coffee. Deliver some cookies. Whatever you do, intentionally be *with* him or her.

The greatest resource you can give is yourself.

**Save the ink industry. Put your pen to work.**

providence

A faith that moves **mountains** is a faith that expands **horizons**. It does not bring us into a **smaller** world full of easy answers but into a **larger** one where there is room for **wonder**.

**Rich Mullins**

Repeating a story multiple times is probably a good sign that it's important. Matthew, Mark, Luke, and John apparently all thought that Jesus turning two fish and fives loaves of bread into enough food for over 5,000 people was pretty significant.

How many of us have ever witnessed something like that? Watching God turn three meals into more than 5,000 just isn't an event in most (read: any) of our lives. We are much more likely to go out and create and work to make the 5,000 meals ourselves. That's what the disciples tried to do when they told Jesus to send the crowds away to go eat. They were so focused on the overwhelming number of people compared to five loaves of bread and two fish that they seemed to forget who was sitting among them. Their only logical reaction was to send away the masses to "'go to the villages and buy themselves some food'" (Matthew 14:15). And often that's our only reaction when faced with needs in life because providing for ourselves is what we know how to do.

But throughout Scripture, God's people are told to trust in God for provision. The account of the Israelites in Exodus is a story of God's people relying on God for deliverance, protection, and even food. As God guides the Israelites out of Egypt and into the desert, the whole community of God's people grumbles to their leaders. They finally reach the point where they wish they had "'died by the LORD's hand in Egypt'" (Exodus 16:3). At least in Egypt they could sit around pots of meat and eat all they wanted.

So what does God do when he hears the Israelites' grumbling? Not unlike turning two fish and five loaves into over 5,000 meals, God tells Moses that he will "'rain down bread from heaven'" (Exodus 16:4) and there will be enough for everyone's needs. God promises to take care of his people, providing their daily bread, each day, every day. Bread falls from the sky and water gushes out of rocks.

We, especially those of us in the United States, have grown accustomed to providing for ourselves. A signifier of a mature adult is the ability to provide for one's own needs. So we work and work and then work some more and maybe do some investing so that we have money and can be sure that all of our needs (and wants) are met. More often than not, we really don't even *need* to trust that God will "rain down bread from heaven" and provide what we need. Most of us can provide for ourselves just fine.

And yet, followers of Christ are to "'look at the birds of the air'" and "'see how the lilies of the field grow'" (Matthew 6:26, 28), abandoning everything and trusting in God alone for provision.

Now this is not to say that we are to quit working and give up all of our responsibilities. After all, Paul tells the Thessalonians that believers should "settle down and earn the bread they eat" (2 Thessalonians 3:12). Work itself is a gift from God and another opportunity to become coworkers with God in his mission of restoration. We must place our work in God's hands and allow him to use it to bless us, our families, and those in need. What's most important is that we trust God to care for us no matter what. Our job is not to gain more for our own security and comfort but to be about the business of God's mission—caring for our families and restoring the poor, the neglected, the hurting, and the world around us. This means relying on God to care for us as we work all we can and give away all we can to love and serve God and others.

A man named John Wesley said something much like this. We will say more about him later, but his philosophy about work and money is worth previewing here. He believed a Christian should earn, save, and give all he or she can. Think about it—earning money to redeem (save) it in order to give it away in acts of love, while trusting God to care for us and make it all possible.

talk

What is the purpose of work?

What is the tension between trusting for provision and being lazy?

Instead of accumulating stuff and money for ourselves, followers of Christ are to **abandon everything**, trusting in God alone for what we need. But that's not always easy. In what situation do you find it hardest to trust God?
What makes it so difficult?

# Provisitation.

## (Anyone can make up words these days.)

God invites us to participate in God's provision for others. We get to accept the invitation.

Prepare a meal for someone in your community—someone sick, or elderly, someone you care for, or even someone you *don't* much care for. Visit them, eat with them, and be part of God's provision for them that day.

**Save the ink industry. Put your pen to work.**

# Our God is an awesome God.

**(hand motions preferred)**

Christian singer and songwriter Rich Mullins built fortune and fame and then gave it all away to love and serve others on a Native American reservation in New Mexico. His life came to a sudden and tragic end in a car accident in 1997. During his life, Mullins challenged followers of Christ to be generous toward others with love and resources and to trust in God for everything.

Explore the life of Rich Mullins online, at your public library, or through *Rich Mullins: A Ragamuffin's Legacy*, a working film about his life. What can you learn from his life of trust, faith, and love?

**Journal your thoughts here.**

# Pray.

Spend the week asking God to reveal the areas of your life that need to be relinquished. Pray that you will be shown the ways that God wants to provide for you. Pray for the courage and support to fully rely on God for all of your needs.

Tell the page what you think.

# Easy or hard?

For some of us, it's easy to ask people for something when we need it. For others, it might feel like a sign of weakness and inadequacy. If you find it easy to ask for things, don't ask right away next time: hold it in prayer and ask God to provide. If it's hard for you to ask, step out a little and ask right away. See how God will provide.

**Artists welcome here. Doodle away.**

# Waiting.

In many ways, we've grown accustomed to providing for ourselves most everything we need in life. Surely God has blessed us with the ability to work and earn resources in order to survive, but maybe we need to be reminded that God is the ultimate provider and sustainer.

Next time you have an urgent need, wait. Instead of rushing to fix it by throwing your emergency fund at it, wait on God, asking him to reveal a plan to you. Imagine what it might be like to not have that emergency fund (which isn't all that difficult for some of us to do!). Sometimes simply waiting on God is what we are asked to do.

**Push a pencil.**

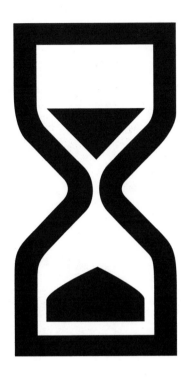

# Total abandonment.

It's written on our money, and we like to think we actually live like it. In God we trust? Or in ourselves and our stuff we trust?

If we're going to trust God with our money, maybe we have to learn to abandon other things first. And maybe it's not even *things* that we have the hardest time releasing. (Or, maybe it is.)

Consider the people, the relationships, in your life that you tend to hold too tightly. Let go. Let this be the first step in abandoning everything and trusting in God alone for provision.

White spaces are meant to be filled.

# Buying new is so overrated.

Whenever we need something, we're quick to run off and buy it at the closest Walmart or Target. Maybe we need a lesson in imagination.

Next time you need something, big or small, see how long you can go by repurposing things or connecting with people. Instead of replacing that broken item or buying something new outright, look for a different way. Do you become more creative when you stop to consider other options?

**Do tell.**

# Nature required.

Go outside. Spend time watching the birds fly around. Look at the flowers and trees blowing in the wind. See how they move and grow in the midst of all creation.

Reflect more on what it means for you to abandon everything and trust God to provide for you in the same way that the birds and flowers are wonderfully cared for.

**Drop a line. Or two.**

mammon

# Starve Mammon with your love.

**Early Church Christian**

Everyone has unique memories from elementary school that seem to stick out among all the others. For instance, I could tell you about the time in fourth grade when I was dancing around the boys' cabin at church camp and fell through the floor—while I wasn't wearing any clothes. But that's probably too long of a story that you aren't really interested in anyway.

There's a word—yeah, I know, not quite as entertaining as the other story—that always seemed fun to me. *Onomatopoeia*. Bang! Boom! Smash! Words that describe a sound. Can't get much more fun, right? Another lesson I remember from fifth grade is the concept of personification: giving human qualities to an object. One of my favorite examples of personification is, "That bacon cheeseburger is calling my name!" Such a lame excuse for eating junk food, right?

Jesus went through school, too. Surely he had an embarrassing moment that could rival my camp experience, and he certainly studied language concepts like onomatopoeia and personification. In Matthew 6, Jesus personifies money itself, giving it a name: Mammon. He says, "'No man can serve two masters: for either he will hate the one, and love the other; or else he will hold to the one, and despise the other. Ye cannot serve God and mammon'" (Matthew 6:24, KJV).

Mammon is the god that we make money to be by structuring life around our cash and shiny plastic cards. It's the god that we serve by overworking ourselves to the point of exhaustion and unbalanced lives, all so that we can enjoy a comfortable lifestyle. Money becomes Mammon when we give it power over our lives—when we choose to store up for ourselves treasures on earth instead of in the kingdom of God. Money becomes Mammon when our eyes are unhealthy and stingy (see Matthew 6:23) and we seek after wealth rather than giving generously.

Maybe we think that as long as we give God ten percent, we're free to do what we please with the rest. But, remember? It's all God's to begin with. When we realize that the key is not just stewardship but *lordship* and allow God to control our pockets, we become cheerful and generous givers and avoid the rule of Mammon in our lives.

talk

Jesus says we can't serve two masters— either we'll hate one and love the other or be devoted to one and despise the other. In what ways do we, both individually and communally, still try to serve both?

Mammon is a force because of the **power we give money**. In what ways do we give power to money? Is it possible to be **free** of the power of Mammon?

# Comparative dissonance.

When Mammon is god, it's easy to fall into comparing ourselves with others. *Man, they sure do have it easy. It must be nice to own that big house and eat out all the time.* We almost always compare up, focusing on those who have *more* than us, and it often leads to envy and coveting.

The next time you notice yourself comparing how much you have with how much others have, stop. Consider the factors causing you to compare. Let it be a reminder to consider whom you serve.

**Do tell.**

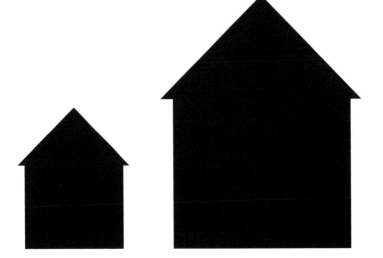

# Huge liquidation! Everything must go!

**(Okay, not really.)**

It's easy to be consumed by the stuff we own. We often fill our days with our computers, TVs, games, social networks, and spending money. But Jesus said life is not measured by what we own (see Luke 12).

Consider the one item in your life that consumes your time and passion, something you can't imagine living without. Don't use it this week. If possible, give it away to someone who needs it. Sometimes simple acts lead us to true worship.

**Journal your thoughts here.**

# Getting personal.

Accountability is like pulling nose hairs. It can tingle a little—or a lot—but it opens up the passageways for life. (Next time, we'll let the experts make the analogies.)

Get together with your group this week. Share a meal, go to coffee, do whatever it is you do. Bring your weekly or monthly budget and pass it around. Keep each other accountable for serving the God of the universe who is worthy of our worship rather than Mammon, the god who steals our joy and love.

Push a pencil.

# Buy more, save more!

**(Um, that makes no sense.)**

Every day we are bombarded with commercials, billboards, and ads that try to convince us to fill our lives with more stuff. Some even promise fulfillment: we know it won't happen but we buy their products anyway.

For one day, keep track of all the ads thrown your way. They're such a huge part of our culture, so chances are you'll miss a few. Be aware as best as possible. Think about their influence on you. Question the product and the message being displayed.

**Artists welcome here. Doodle away.**

# Eating humble pie.

## (Most prefer to stick with pumpkin.)

It's easy to *say* we serve God over Mammon. It's also easy to trick ourselves.

Have somebody close to you track your life for the week. This person will record what you do, who you spend your time with, where you hang out, what you spend your resources on. Does another person's perspective of whom or what you serve line up with yours?

**Tell the page what you think.**

# Frivolous spender or penny-pincher?

Whether money burns a whole in your pocket or you deposit loose change into your checking account, it's important to examine your spending habits.

Keep a strict record of every penny you spend this week on gas, coffee, groceries, clothes, donations, movie tickets, snacks, rent... everything. How much of your spending is necessary (like, really *necessary*)? How much is on extras? Reflect on what your spending says about whom you serve.

White spaces are meant to be filled.

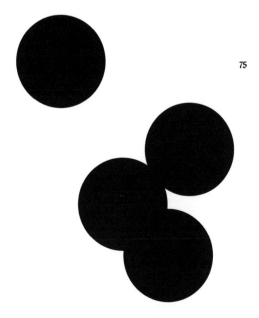

# I'm not that rich!

Even though we often compare ourselves to the people who have more than we do, where do we really sit on the money line?

Go to www.globalrichlist.com and find out how rich you actually are. Share your reaction, whatever it is, with a friend.

**Drop a line. Or two.**

# Convinced that enough is not enough.

The love of God that Christians seek to imitate is a selfless, self-giving love. But it's easier to talk about than to live out.

This week, be aware of the thoughts and actions that reflect the selfish desires for more—more money, more stuff, more fortune. When you are convincing yourself that what you have is actually not enough, recommit to denouncing earthly treasures and, instead, storing up treasures for the kingdom of God.

**Save the ink industry. Put your pen to work.**

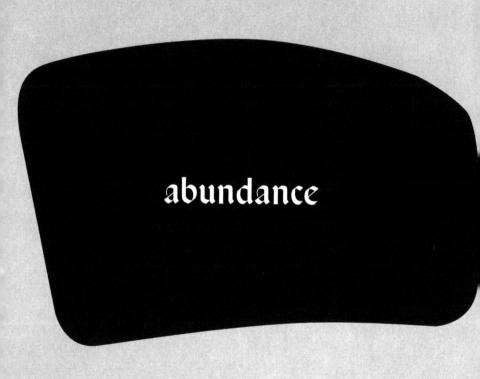

abundance

There is enough for everyone's **need** but not enough for everyone's **greed.**

**Gandhi**

Sometimes people say things that leave us utterly confused. Such is the case for Nicodemus when he approaches Jesus at night in John 3:1-21. Nicodemus simply wants to understand Jesus, who he is, and how and why he is doing things like turning water into wine (see John 2:1-11) and flipping over tables as he drives money-changers out of God's temple (see John 2:12-25). Jesus wastes no time telling Nicodemus that one must be born again to see the kingdom of God. "'How can a man be born when he is old?' Nicodemus ask[s]. 'Surely he cannot enter a second time into his mother's womb to be born!'" (John 3:4). Born again. New creation. Participant of a new kingdom that is breaking into this world. These concepts were completely foreign to Nicodemus.

This new allegiance—to the king and his kingdom rather than to kingdoms of the world—reveals practices and habits that perhaps we have never thought about. We realize that the kingdom belongs to the least of these (see Matthew 5:3, 25:31-46) and our lives should lead us to encounter the poor, sick, lonely, and forgotten instead of the worldly tendency to focus on ourselves. We realize that our rebirth is a birth into a heavenly family that has no national borders—and being part of a kingdom with no national borders might cause us to rethink violence against other nations. As family members of the kingdom of God, we consider how what we spend our money on affects children and people around the world who work as slaves to produce what we buy.

Our ultimate allegiance is to the kingdom of God, and God's way confronts the very patterns of this world—patterns of selfishness, nationalism, individualism, and materialism. The Church is to show a different way—God's way. Because in a world where one percent of us own half the world's money, we need God's way.

What might Jesus say about this brokenness when it comes to God's resources? In Luke 12:15, Jesus says, "'Beware! Guard against every kind of greed. Life is not measured by how much you own'" (*NLT*). Then (again, Jesus was apt to do this), he tells a story about a rich man whose business has provided him with so many possessions, he doesn't know where to put them all. So he decides,

"This is what I'll do. I will tear down my barns and build bigger ones, and there I will store all my grain and my goods. And I'll say to myself, 'You have plenty of good things laid up for many years. Take life easy; eat, drink and be merry.'" (Luke 12:18-19)

Jesus says God sees the man and isn't pleased: "'You fool! This very night your life will be demanded from you. Then who will get what you have prepared for yourself'" (verse 20)? Jesus ends the teaching by explaining that this is how things will end for all of us who store up stuff for ourselves (verse 21).

Maybe Jesus is imagining a different way to live—a way in which instead of storing up for ourselves, we care for those without. It's weird—it's a new and different way—to not store up for ourselves. But as kingdom people, we give ourselves to God's kingdom of self-sacrificial love, and we dream of ways to love others with our resources instead of hoarding them for ourselves.

talk

Jesus's story was about crops and barns because he told stories his listeners could relate to. If Jesus told the same story today, what might the "crops" and "barns" be?

If **Jesus** says that storing things up for ourselves ends **poorly**, is there a certain amount that is still okay to store up? What are some alternatives to **storing** our money and resources?

# BOGO of a different kind.

Next time you buy something new, give away a similar item. Buy one, give one. Maybe you're buying a new coat—give a coat in your closet away. Buying something that you don't already have? Buy two and give one away to someone in need.

**Push a pencil.**

# For those with an open mind.

Singer-songwriter Derek Webb is known for his songs that often push Christians outside of their comfort zone, challenging us to re-think our lives around the life of Christ. Some people love his stuff. Others... not so much.

Listen to Webb's song "Rich Young Ruler." Look up the lyrics if it helps. Write one thing you like, one thing you don't like, and one thing you feel challenged by in the song. Consider this a practice of thinking outside the box with your abundance.

**Journal your thoughts here.**

# More than just a trend.

Storage buildings in the United States make up a $20+ billion industry. It is considered "recession resistant" based on its performance since the downfall of the economy in 2008.[2] Even in what the U.S. considers a crisis, we here in the U.S. are still storing *a lot* of stuff.

Whether you have enough stuff to fill your whole house *and* a storage unit, or just your garage, or just your closets, or just your desks, chances are you have an abundance of stuff lying around. "Simplify" has become a trendy word in some circles, but Jesus said that life is not measured by what we own. Maybe, then, simplifying should be more than just a trend.

Go through all of your "stuff," especially stuff that's just gathering dust. Sell it or give it to someone who can actually use it. Enjoy the gift of less.

Do tell.

# Did JB really mean that?

For some of us, the biggest indicator of our abundance is our closet. John the Baptist said, "'If you have two coats, give one away'" (Luke 3:11, *MSG*). But what if we have *ten*?

Take a hard look at your closet. Does the abundance show? Pull out some clothes you no longer wear (or perhaps never wore). If you are really serious, take out some you do wear. Donate to a local shelter or to someone you know who needs them.

What more can you do to live a one-shirt lifestyle?

**Save the ink industry. Put your pen to work.**

# Selling other people's stuff. Not normally recommended.

For various reasons, some storage units get left behind and all the contents are often just taken to the dump. Contact a local storage unit company and ask them what their policy is on units that have been abandoned. Volunteer to clean out a unit or two, and be creative with what you do with the stuff. Sell it, use it, give it away. Be resourceful. Resist taking stuff to the dump.

**White spaces are meant to be filled.**

FOR SALE

# Maintaining the surplus.

Imagine the fun and memories having a financial surplus could bring.
A boat. A lake house. A cabin. A Mini Cooper.

Interview a friend who owns something you've always dreamed
of having, something that would increase the fun in life. Estimate
the dollars per hour necessary to maintain the boat, the cabin, or
vacation home, the luxury automobile. Has it been worth the cost,
the maintenance, and travel?

**Artists welcome here. Doodle away.**

# Hey neighbor, can I use the lawn mower?

Maybe they'll go for it; maybe they won't. It doesn't hurt to ask.

Talk to your neighbors (you might have to get to know them first!) about sharing a lawn mower, weed trimmer, and other yard equipment among all of you. Talk about the savings in cost and the details of how it would work. Enjoy the future conversations with your neighbors.

Don't need your mower anymore? Sell it on Craigslist and give the money to an organization or person in need you care about.

**Tell the page what you think.**

# Cutting the cable.

Jesus's words cause us to reconsider the "extras" in our lives to which we give God's money. We are forced to question if the money is going to people and places that need it most.

Cable or satellite TV is one of those extras. Weigh the pros and cons of getting rid of it: chances are you can find most of your shows online. Not having it might even help you connect with other people as you join them to watch the big game or your favorite show.

If you don't have cable TV, reflect on other extras that you might cut out.

**Drop a line. Or two.**

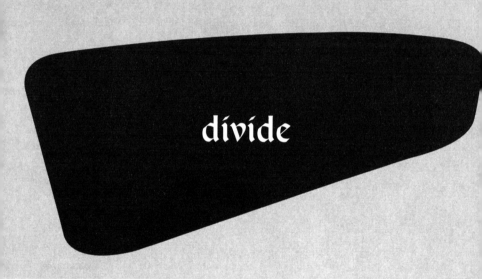

divide

I'm convinced that God did not mess up and make too many people and not enough stuff. Poverty was created not by God but by **you and me**, because we have not learned to **love** our neighbors as ourselves.

## Shane Claiborne

Somewhere along the line, some of us seem to have convinced ourselves that God created some people rich and others poor. Or at least we have lived like it. But from Old Testament to New, we see a God who advocates for the "have-nots" and admonishes the "haves" to give to those who are in need. Laws such as Jubilee and gleaning, among others, were put in place centuries ago to ensure that the Israelites cared for the poor among them (see Leviticus 25). Jesus says the poor are blessed and the kingdom of God belongs to them (see Matthew 5:3; Luke 6:20). He tells one man that he must sell everything and give it to the poor in order to be born again (see Matthew 19:16-22; Mark 10:17-27). And Scripture repeatedly offers woes to the rich, instructing them to rid themselves of wealth so that they may care for the poor (see Luke 6:24; James 5:1-6). And yet, we seem to have largely ignored the 2,000-plus verses in Scripture that reveal a God who loves and provides for the poor and vulnerable and calls his followers to do the same.

Maybe it's because many of us have been brought up in a country that spends half of its budget on military while its people sleep on the streets. Maybe it's because we're part of a society that puts worth in possessions, a society where enough is never actually enough, a society that blames the poor for their own poverty. Maybe it's because we measure our wealth against the mega-rich, the CEO, the celebrity, and the professional athlete. Maybe it's because we have insulated ourselves from ever having to directly interact with the poor, choosing instead to offer our charity to organizations that do the work for us.

You get the point. We have built walls, both metaphorically and literally, that divide us from the poor and from having to take responsibility for the reality that some are dying of starvation and thirst while others (we) live comfortably in riches. If we are to play a role in the redemptive mission of God, if we are to be the hands and feet of Jesus, we can't pretend that we can do whatever we please with our money while others live in poverty.

talk

Jesus talked a lot(!) about the poor, broken, and downtrodden. Are you comfortable with talking about our need to love, serve, and give to the poor? What keeps us from doing this more?

We spend $5 for our favorite cup of coffee and our churches build multi-million-dollar additions while **people** around the world die from lack of food, water, and shelter. As followers of Christ, what is our **responsibility** to the poor? Are we justified in spending on luxuries while others **suffer**?

# I'll take some conversation with that sandwich.

Grab a friend and prepare a picnic basket (blanket and all if you so desire). Head to a city park and invite a homeless friend or two to eat with you. Listen to their story—sometimes they need someone to talk to more than anything. Share your food and your love.

**White spaces are meant to be filled.**

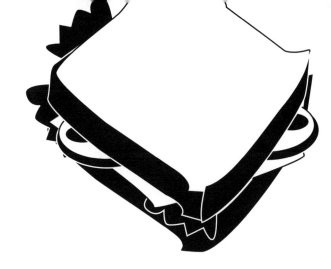

# Chef wish list.

Rescue missions and homeless shelters provide thousands of meals each month, and they often depend on donations and gifts for their food resources. Go down to your local shelter or mission. Meet the chef and find out what is on his or her wish list. Chances are you can provide a couple items to keep the food tasty.

**Save the ink industry. Put your pen to work.**

# Not that buildings are bad, but...

The early prophets would say that a church that spends millions of dollars on buildings while her children are starving is guilty of murder. While we build our temples, human temples are being destroyed by hunger and homelessness.[3]

Request to view your church's annual budget. Talk to your pastor or church leaders about how the money is being spent. Is it going toward God's kingdom of justice and compassion? Seek to understand and offer grace, but don't be afraid to ask questions.

Drop a line. Or two.

# Making room for the other.

Reuben Welch once defined hospitality as opening up a space in your heart to make room for someone else. We're going to take the liberty to add to his definition.

Consider what it would be like to not just open up your heart to outsiders but to open up your *home*. Millions of people eat their meals (when they have them) on the streets alone because they have no family or friends to eat with and talk to. Get to know one of these people and invite them into your home for a meal. Take a risk. Be hospitable.

**Journal your thoughts here.**

# Going diving.

**This one's for the courageous.**

Instead of going through the drive-through or scanning the refrigerator, find a meal out of a dumpster. Be wise about it: pick a dumpster close to a grocery store or a restaurant. Hey, with all the food being thrown out every day, we bet you'll find more than one meal. Experience what it's like to not know where your next meal is going to come from and when you will eat again.

**Do tell.**

# Don't you remember what you learned in preschool?

**It's good to share.**

This month, set aside part of your grocery budget. See how far you can make your money go when you buy only what you really need. Use the money you set aside to make a large meal for those without food. Take the meal to the park and pass it out, spending time talking to those you're feeding.

Another option: Ask restaurants to donate some food for you to take to the hungry.

**Push a pencil.**

# Oh, the things we take for granted.

Most of us will never truly know what it's like to be hungry. *Really* hungry, not the afternoon hankering for some chips.

In whatever way is best for you, choose to fast from food this week. Maybe one meal a day. Maybe two whole days. Let your hunger be a reminder to pray for and serve those who are without food.

**Tell the page what you think.**

# You may need a bulldozer.

We don't always consciously erect walls that separate us from the poor and needy. Walls are often built simply when we follow the routines of our everyday lives.

Identify the walls between you and the poor. How many are there? How can you knock them down? If, for some reason, you can't be in direct relationship with the poor, find out if there is anyone you know who is and how you can help in this individual's or group's work.

**Artists welcome here. Doodle away.**

systems

We are not to simply bandage the wounds of victims beneath the **wheels of injustice**, but we are to **drive a spoke** into the wheel itself.

## Dietrich Bonhoeffer

I was born in Colorado to a family who loved and supported me (and still does). My family didn't have as much as some, but I was always well fed, had clothes to wear (even though I had to resort to creating my own Nike socks using a black permanent marker), attended school, and even got to go to some Rockies baseball games. I had everything I needed. I was born into a system that didn't hinder my ability to live.

Javier, one of the children my wife and I get to sponsor, was born in Honduras and has lived a life completely different from mine. Food is scarce, his clothes are torn, and he just started getting some education. Javier rarely has everything he needs. He was born into a system that requires him to fight for his life.

There are systems everywhere. From who can vote, to who can go to school, to who can get a lunch at the rescue mission, to who can get a place to live, systems are interwoven into our lives. Neither Javier nor I *chose* to be born into the places and systems of our lives. Nobody chooses. Somehow, we seem to have forgotten this fact. We have become indifferent to injustice. It's not easy to see people sleeping under a bridge, but it's easier to look away than to ask what could be done to fix the problem. It's not easy to see pictures online of starving children in developing countries, but it's easier to click away than to be a part of the change. It takes time, energy, and resources to invest ourselves into working with God to rid the world of injustice. And all too often we convince ourselves that we don't have enough time, energy, and resources to make a difference. So we turn away and hope that someone else will do something.

It's also not easy to look critically at the systems in our own lives that create habitual spending of money. Even as we begin to be more intentional with money, we find ourselves spending money on things just because it's *normal* to do so. Lattes and smartphones come to mind.

Not all systems are bad. It's when a system results in some being rich and others living on the streets that the Church has a responsibility to cry out. Injustice has no place in the coming kingdom of God. It should have no place in our world today.

There will always be systems at work in our lives. Some we choose. Some we don't. And some we can work with God to dismantle so that our world may be restored to its intended wholeness.

talk

What systems involving money and resources oppress people? What systems lead to habits of unnecessary spending? What systems serve and care for the oppressed?

It's often easy to assume our **governments** will care for the **oppressed.** But then we might wonder if governments are always interested in that job and if they're doing **more harm than good.** What is the relationship, if any, between what the Church is **called** to, and governments' involvement in that call?

# Dumbing down.

Waiting for your next cell phone upgrade? Already own an expensive smartphone? Maybe it's better to be dumb. We often spend money on stuff just because it's normal in our culture to do so. But do we really need the expensive luxuries that a smartphone offers?

As a small attempt to disable a consumeristic system in America, decide to "dumb down" instead of upgrading to the best smartphone on the market. Spend the money that you would be spending each month on a cell phone on something of greater importance.

**Artists welcome here. Doodle away.**

# The gift of life. Literally.

Chances are, you have a warm home, a comfortable bed, and a refrigerator full of food. And chances (well, no, it's a pretty sure thing) are, you didn't *choose* to be born into a family with your needs already met and the opportunity to continue to thrive. You are fortunate. Others aren't.

Hundreds of millions of children around the world struggle each day, simply because they don't have opportunity to thrive and grow. Some struggle to find food and water. Others struggle for the opportunity to learn and gain an education. And others struggle due to lack of available healthcare. Child sponsorship provides these basic needs to children around the world.

Look up child sponsorship organizations (Nazarene Compassionate Ministries and World Vision are two excellent options), and commit to sponsoring a child (or more than one). Make it more than just sending money: pray for your child, send letters and small gifts. Some organizations even allow sponsors to visit the children they're helping to support.

**Push a pencil.**

# Maybe a choice…but probably not.

It's easy to become skeptical of people who are in poverty. But we often don't even seek to understand how they got there in the first place.

Seek to understand. Talk to some people in your community who are working every day with the poor and homeless. Find out what factors contribute to people living and staying in poverty. Ask about the hearts of the people they help.

Better yet, go straight to the poor. Hear their stories. How did they end up where they are? What are their dreams and goals?

White spaces are meant to be filled.

# A system that works.

An organization with an almost 99 percent success rate is one to get behind, especially when their mission is to alleviate poverty and create opportunities around the world.

Kiva is an organization with just that mission. You make a loan to someone who needs it. The loan recipient earns money and pays you back so that you can do it again. Kiva has a 98.5 percent repayment rate!

Go to www.kiva.org. Explore the needs, how it works, and how you can give. Make a loan or two. Stay involved as you get progress updates on your loan and whom it is helping.

**Tell the page what you think.**

# The shoe that grows.

It's fun to buy cool shoes for ourselves and know that a child in another country is also getting a pair of shoes (www.toms.com). But what happens when that child outgrows the shoes?

That's where Because International comes in. Because International is building a shoe that actually grows as kids' feet grow. Go to their website, www.becauseinternational.com. See what they're doing and how you can get involved in relieving poverty around the world.

**Journal your thoughts here.**

# No hands but yours.
# No feet but mine.

We often wonder and question why God doesn't just eliminate poverty and evil in the world. Why doesn't God do something to stop all of it? God did. He created you. We are God's hands and feet, working with and for God to restore the world.

Go to YouTube and watch "Depraved Indifference" by Eric Ludy. What challenges you? What rubs you the wrong way? Reflect on what it means to be the hands and feet of Christ.

Save the ink industry. Put your pen to work.

# Plenty to choose from.

Basically everything we spend our money on has in some way been affected by an unjust system. We often aren't aware of the slavery and violence that are part of our everyday lives, crying out in the clothes we buy, the coffee we drink, or the products we consume.

From child slavery, to human and drug trafficking, to the sex trade, the list goes on from there. Research and take a stand against a system that creates inequity. Commit to spending money at businesses that are not part of the injustice.

**Drop a line. Or two.**

# Occupy local.

It doesn't really matter whether we all fully agree with the "Occupy" movements. The fact that six Walmart heirs possess wealth equal to that of the bottom 30 percent[4] should cause us to stop and think how we are contributing. We can't just ignore the realities that are causing some to suffer.

Shopping at local stores helps sustain your community and those who live in it. Shop locally this month. Be creative if you find it's a little more expensive. Don't take the easy way out.

Already shopping locally? Make it a point to encourage others to do the same.

**Do tell.**

given

Justice and mercy are not **add-ons** to worship, nor are they the consequences of worship. Justice and mercy are **intrinsic** to God and therefore intrinsic to the worship of God.

**Mark Labberton**

In a race-to-the-top and build-wealth-at-all-costs world, it's easy for the Church to lose its prophetic voice. A Church that is called to exemplify a new world, a new way, a new kingdom, has often forgotten that it follows a king who washes his disciples' feet with a towel, proclaiming that the Christian life is a race to the bottom. The first shall be last and the last shall be first. Do we truly believe it?

We may struggle to believe Jesus's words sometimes, which is why it's important to look at the lives of people by whose examples we can live. John Wesley, one of the founders of Methodism and a well-known theologian of the 18th century, said, "If I leave behind me ten pounds (currently about $20) [when I die]... you and all mankind bear witness against me, that I have lived and died a thief and a robber." Wesley believed there wasn't anything wrong with making money as long as we spend all of it helping the poor, after supplying for one's own needs and the needs of family. He couldn't fathom how one could spend money on luxuries while others suffered in poverty. Wesley practiced what he preached: his net worth when he died was about thirty bucks. The only money mentioned in his will was the random coins lost in pockets and dresser drawers.[5] For Wesley, it was a given that our resources are intended to go to those who need them most.

Jesus believed it was a given as well. Yes, Jesus believed it was a *given* that we pass our money on to the poor:
> "So when you give to the needy, do not announce it with trumpets, as the hypocrites do in the synagogues and on the streets, to be honored by men. I tell you the truth, they have received their reward in full. But when you give to the needy, do not let your left hand know what your right hand is doing." (Matthew 6:2-3)

In many ways, we seem to have swapped Jesus's "when" with our "if". *If* we give to the needy... It's no longer a given that Christians and churches support the poor. We've lost God's way.

The Church must regain its prophetic voice in the world, shouting from the mountaintops that the rich are to give to the poor out of worship (see 1 Timothy 6:17-19). May we shout with our lives and with humility, grasping the towel of Jesus as we serve the world.

talk

John Wesley strongly believed that the Church is to care for the poor. What do you think of his claim that to die with money saved was to rob from God and those who need it most?

Jesus said to give in **secret**—that we might not even **know** we are giving to the needy (that whole left hand, right hand thing). What challenges do we face in making our giving to the needy in secret?

# Earn all you can, save all you can, give all you can.

John Wesley's philosophy of money came down to this: Earn all you can, save all you can, give all you can. How am I supposed to give all I can if I'm saving all I can? Seems a little contradictory, eh?

Go to http://tinyurl.com/bvqjc2b and read through Wesley's sermon "The Use of Money" to get a better idea of what he means. Share it with a friend. And pardon Wesley's old-school English.

**Save the ink industry. Put your pen to work.**

# Scrubbing toilets can be fun.

It's easy to become short-sighted when volunteering. We can fall into doing acts of compassion because it makes us feel good. But if we're serving people simply because we are supposed to and it makes us feel good, we might be doing it wrong.

The next time you volunteer to serve, whether it's at the local rescue mission, Salvation Army, or elsewhere, let the leaders know that you are there to do *whatever needs to be done.* Be ready for anything. Serve with love and compassion.

**Do tell.**

155

# Simple but not easy.

Mother Teresa said, "Following Jesus is simple but not easy. Love until it hurts, and then love more." Love encompasses giving. Give until it hurts, and then give more. Give your resources, your energy, your time, your heart, yourself.

Spend some time contemplating these words. Ask God to give you God's heart for people.

**Drop a line. Or two.**

# It's just like your comfy room. Except not so much.

Giving our resources and ourselves to the needy becomes part of who we are when we truly understand the lives of those to whom we're giving. Compassion is driven by placing ourselves in the other's shoes.

Spend a night, or a week if you're able, in a homeless shelter or under a bridge. Be aware of your tendencies to take things for granted, but make it more about others than about yourself. What does your experience teach you about giving and serving?

**Tell the page what you think.**

159

# Can I get a to-go box, please?

It's easy to forget that while we are out eating burgers and bottomless fries, people are hungry right outside.

Next time you go out to eat, whether you're eating fast-food or something a little fancier, buy an extra meal to go and give it to someone on the street. Think about what it would require for you to make this a habit.

**Artists welcome here.**
**Doodle away.**

# Moving into Jesus's neighborhood.

The goal isn't to just throw our money at the poor. Giving money and resources is valuable and is part of the journey toward eliminating poverty, but it's not the whole picture. We must learn to live incarnationally among the marginalized. That's hard to do when we've moved out of their neighborhoods.

Think about the location of your house. Are you living among the needy? Do you encounter the poor? Maybe you can't move to a different part of town (or maybe you can), but take the necessary steps to "move into the neighborhoods" of Christ; he is found among the outcast and unloved.

White spaces are meant to be filled.

# Nothing New November.

Or whatever next month is.

Go an entire month without buying anything new, beyond what you *need*.

**Push a pencil.**

# Got enough tubes of toothpaste there, crazy coupon lady?

Maybe you love to coupon. You love searching the ads and looking for crazy deals. Or maybe you simply like the idea of stretching your resources, especially to help others.

Toothpaste, toothbrushes, shampoo, soap, and deodorant are some of the most-needed items at rescue missions and shelters. They also happen to be some of the items that you can get the most of for just a couple dollars—if you coupon correctly. Buy some of these necessities, stretching your money as far as possible, and deliver them to those who need them.

**Journal your thoughts here.**

community

There were no **needy** persons among them.

**Acts 4:34**

My seven-year-old niece loves to draw all sorts of pictures. My favorites are her unicorns. She just makes them look so... real. If my niece were to draw some images and numbers on a piece of paper, that single piece of paper probably wouldn't be worth much more than the picture of a unicorn she recently gave me. But for some reason, we give a lot of power to some smashed up pulpwood that has little pictures and various numbers printed on it. With the power that we give to money, it often becomes Mammon, the god we serve when our focus turns from God to goods.

Jesus seems to take this idea that money has power and turns it on its head. He basically says, "Use money to make friends, to build relationships, because that's about all it's good for" (see Luke 16:9).[6] And in the early Church, we see a community of people who make friends with their money, pooling together their money and resources: "No one claimed that any of his possessions was his own, but they shared everything they had" (Acts 4:32). They were content with food and clothing (see 1 Timothy 6:8). The amazing result of this practice was that "there were no needy persons among them" (Acts 4:34).

Apparently, it *is* possible to eliminate poverty.

The Church today, maybe especially the Church in the United States, has come a long way from the early Church. And rightly so. We aren't called to be the early Church; we're called to be the 21st century Church. But that doesn't mean we don't have anything to learn from the early Christians, those who lived so closely to the life and person of Jesus of Nazareth.

In a world of iPods, iPads, iPhones, and iLife, individualism reigns king. Looking out for "number one" and not giving a second thought to how we can love our neighbor with our money, we have largely forgotten the inter-connectedness that we have been created to live in and need. As we look back at the loving community of the early Christians, we recognize how far we have come from the community for which God created us and the community that proclaimed there is enough for everyone.

We don't have to be the early Church, but today's Church is still called to be a weird *community*, showing the rest of the world how to once again live in God's ways. We need people and churches who will humbly offer a new way that counters individualism with love and sharing. Pooling our resources and money together in order to distribute to those in need doesn't make sense to the world (it likely doesn't even make sense to most of us). But as we learn to love our neighbor as ourselves as the world watches, maybe that's not such a bad thing.

talk

The early Church was known for sharing everything they had. What would it look like, in our day and age, for the Church to share possessions and money?

The idea of sharing **everything** definitely feels weird and maybe even **offensive** to some of us. What is exciting to you about the idea? What causes fear and frustration?

# Because there is enough for everyone.

Relational Tithe (www.relationaltithe.com) is a global community of people committed to meeting the needs of others. Needs are posted and met by people around the world. Head to their website: ponder the concept, explore, meet others, share ideas, get involved.

**Tell the page what you think.**

# Not your typical potluck

I tell myself I won't eat too much, but that gumbo always gets me at the church potluck.

Plan a church potluck lunch. Maybe it's for the whole church, or maybe it's for your small group and some others. Instead of the classic everyone-brings-whatever-they-want style potluck, cook up enough beans and rice for everyone. Think about collecting some money to be given to the hungry. Talk about the experience.

**White spaces are meant to be filled.**

# Feel free to conspire.

Is Jesus really the reason for the season? We say he is, but often our materialistic culture gets the best of us at Christmas time. The time of year when it should be easiest to worship Jesus often becomes the hardest as we fill our lives with Christmas lists, running from store to store, and buying a bunch of *things*.

Go to www.adventconspiracy.org and explore this resource that enables communities to leave behind the religion of consumerism and enter into the story of Christmas. Talk to your church leaders about participating in Advent Conspiracy next Advent.

**Push a pencil.**

# But I thought God liked our music...

"'I hate, I despise your religious feasts; I cannot stand your assemblies'"… "'Away with the noise of your songs! I will not listen to the music of your harps.'" These are God's strong words to the Israelites in the book of Amos (5:21, 23). But in verse 24 he continues, "'But let justice roll on like a river, righteousness like a never-failing stream!'"

Read Amos 5:21-24 every day this week with one or two other people. Make a list of five tangible things your community can do to let justice roll and righteousness flow.

**Artists welcome here. Doodle away.**

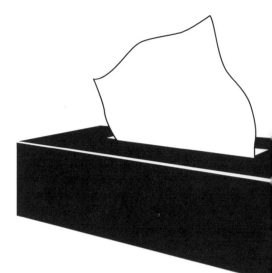

# Disinfectant wipes are a plus.

Families might be able to afford the new clothes and toys for their growing children. Maybe not. Either way, maybe there's a better way than everyone buying a bunch of new stuff.

Consider the families in your church and community. Start a program that allows families to share and trade clothes, toys, and resources. Ask a web expert to develop a simple website where families can post needs and items are ready to be shared.

**Drop a line. Or two.**

# We actually think people shouldn't be dying of hunger.

Every day, hunger kills as many as 11,000 kids under age five. Every day. Eleven *thousand* kids. Think about that for a minute. Hunger is man-made.

Go to www.30hourfamine.org. View the resources that are available in order for your group and community to become more aware of hunger around the world. Set some dates to participate, and invite as many people as you can to be involved in the fight to overcome hunger.

Do tell.

# Break a leg? We've got your back.

Many Christ-followers are searching for alternatives to the ways of the world. They're seeking community and spending resources in ways that contribute to God's mission.

One part of life that thousands of Christians have re-imagined is healthcare. (It's a touchy subject, we know.) Research the alternatives that Christians have come up with pertaining to healthcare. Christian Healthcare Ministries and Samaritan Ministries International are two to start with.

Whether you simply become more knowledgeable of other options or decide to jump in and try the alternatives, reflect on how Christians can share burdens.

**Journal your thoughts here.**

# Speak up.

In the culture we've created, we've often made it difficult for people to speak up. Whether one is in need of help or has the means to help, some are fearful of the response they'll receive when asking or giving. This isn't exactly the culture we see in the early Church.

Think about the culture of your church and community. Help create an environment that ensures that givers and receivers maintain their dignity as a valuable part of the community, no matter their economic standing.

**Save the ink industry. Put your pen to work.**

189

endnotes